Stem of Us

Stem of
Us

poems

Carter McKenzie

Stem of Us
Copyright © 2018 Carter McKenzie

Author photo by Paul Dix

First Flowstone Press Edition • May 2018
ISBN 978-1-945824-16-6

Barbara Kingsolver excerpt from "In Exile" from
Another America: Otra America. Copyright © 1992 by Barbara Kingsolver.
Reprinted with permission of The Frances Goldin Literary Agency.

Li-Young Lee excerpt from "Hurry toward Beginning" from
Book of My Nights. Copyright © 2001 by Li-Young Lee. Reprinted
with the permission of The Permissions Company, Inc.,
on behalf of BOA Editions, Ltd., www.boaeditions.org.

Cover and flower images throughout courtesy
Hervé Sauquet & Jürg Schönenberger

The original source for these images is from their paper
"The ancestral flower of angiosperms and its early diversification,"
by Hervé Sauquet, et al. published in the journal
Nature Communications, online 1 August 2017.

Read the full study at
https://www.nature.com/articles/ncomms16047

To Ryan and Eavan

To know you
is to learn to resist the beauty
of the single red rose in a glass.
It could belong on my table
were it not for roots and leaves,
the possibility of fruit,
the stem
that is only cut once.

—Barbara Kingsolver, from "In Exile"
Another America: Otra America

* * *

When will I be born? Am I the flower,
wide awake inside the falling fruit?

—Li-Young Lee, from "Hurry toward Beginning"
Book of My Nights

Table of Contents

STEM OF WORDS

My First Muse Was Earth	3
Gift in Childhood	4
Translation	5
Christmas, 1962	7
Before Nightfall	9
The End of Beauty	11
Canvas as Portal	12

STEM OF SILENCE

Creation Story	17
Mike	18
Unspoken	21
In the Midst of Place, Thoughts on Juneteenth	23
Armband Chorus of the American Dream	26
Shriek	28
To You Who Found My Brother	29
Traveling	30
The Coffin of Emmett Till	32

STEM OF NESTS

Demeter in November	37
Nest	38
November Return	40
Migration in Changing Climates	41
An Aspect of Theater	43
Subject Matter	45
Parvin Butte	47
Volatilization in Cedar Valley	49
Drowning in Space	51

STEM OF BELONGINGS

Praise Songs for a House	57
Keeping the Fires	59
Ekphrasis	60
Waking Vision	61
Belonging	62
What Stays	63
Witness of Roses	64

STEM OF PRAYERS

poem in the dark	71
Prayer for the Black Bears, Lost Valley	73
Stories of the Black Ware Seed Jar	74
The Possible Stories of Trees	76
What Must Be True	78
To Be Greeted at the River	81
Prayer for Heaven	84

Stem of Words

My first muse was earth

amber stone beneath
a river or a creek

      remnant of tree and air—

this was before I knew
histories
of snow—
my eyes
were hungry
and unafraid

      I saw fire
when the water surprised me
with its sting and its ache—

      that flickering beast—
alive alive
eating my feet to the ankles
with its freezing teeth—

the wind in the pines
carried on
in my dreams, and I

reached for that dark,
called it
singing—

Gift in Childhood

how a word might mean a self
of sounds, vowels, grounded, opening
around the stem of a way to be

what had been drawn from earth
and roots and water, the river
rushing against the stones, the mountain

the bright river, source
of her new word

that marvelous turning

after the bright river

Translation

earth and air
in the word

brief
inhabitance

necessary
the shift of line
the shift of light

the instinct of breath

how it meant
winter, spring, the calendar
of a child

a reading of ice and dust

transparency
of mind and hand

before the sky closed
again, imperceptibly
over the mountains

leaving cloud-shadows
rough edges

on the page
a trace of life
moving

for its own sake

Christmas, 1962

She learns early
(invisible)
age two

    covered neck-to-toe
    in red flannel, red of hearth, red of candle, a bright sled
        with its little rope,
    its silent passages of snow

    and she this moment,
    her new-walking feet, tucked
    into warmth

before the black-and-white set,
an accordion buzzing
for the last show

    before the dial clicks *off*

    an accident, a sudden
    goodnight kiss
    from her and she is brushed aside

    but no
    word for it yet and she removed, and folded up
inside her chest

      little bird of shame
gone somewhere to learn a lesson

shepherds and kings

keeping watch in the fields

Before Nightfall

I hear the pace of leaves
parting, the steps, a slow approach just now, deer
making their way up the hill below my house
through madrone, cedar, and fir,
through poison oak and blackberry bramble
and the soft grasses, and I cannot see but know
      it could be any woods just now, it could be
mule deer making their way among aspen
when I was a child, trees
I cannot see but know
are gold in broad daylight
in the autumn, like it is now,
are gold against the mountains,
against the blue over entirely different mountains
remote and gray
      it could be any woods and any deer,
making their way up the road
to my mother's childhood home
in the Blue Ridge mountains,
the barn where Black Beauty slept
year after year until she was simply gone,
where wasps made their nests, and the deer
made their way to feed off the garden
of my grandmother's early mornings
before the heat and mosquitoes set in
just as these black-tailed deer now feed off the pale-green
      lichen
and berries and fallen apples of this Cascade range
      this Northwestern place,
      which makes me think

of Mechunk Creek, Appalachian waters,
swimming holes and fishing spots for my mother
and her brother, *Mechunk* like the sound of a stone
landing in an echoing body
at the bottom of a well, a stone
      you will never see again, once-bright, and how I watched
my younger brother and sisters come back from the woods
with a bucket of catfish, singing, then fighting over
who caught the fish,
      that picture of my brother's
      huge eyes and his skinny chest,
      which makes me think of the crow with the broken wing
saved by a child who would not be saved in his
twenty-second year, my mother's brother,
      the abandoned shelter
of doghouses, frayed burlap nailed to the entrances
      how the dog I knew
by the name of Scarlet though no one else remembers that name
curled by the fire and allowed me to rest my head on her side
      and I know it
could be any woods, whole regions
now, in half-light, a habitation of pitch-black trunks
of white oak trees, transparencies,
which make me think of a children's book,
a book I can no longer find
      pictures of a mother and daughter
      crossing a bridge near a well-lit house,
      and how the sky deepens
to cobalt and blue-black behind the trees,
how the woods reveal themselves
      just like this, near what I know are the approaching deer,
in the Cascades, here, near Lost Creek, a path to the river
among trees I do and do not recognize.

The End of Beauty

like lost prayer beads they fell
through my fingers
through air defining steps
beneath my feet
negative spaces
tapping palms and wrists
resistant
what I could not hold, the not-holding
itself becoming
my attention, a gathering
the dark horse the point
the fracture the unbidden sky
a field of electric
attractions, rejections, the work
I could not see being born

Canvas as Portal

rim of blue like the path of the mountains

opening to path-
receptions

negative space
the shape of the path breaking

ground of blue into light

attentive to branches
what they become out of the rising

that could drown
any minute

possible roots and leaves

    the moon going on meanwhile
silvering the grasses

with her waxing and waning

    the brush of that

Stem of Silence

Creation Story

The law of the mind longs for blossoms. Camas lilies like a
rumor in the green field, cumulative suggestions; wild iris
this season, sheer life, thriving in the slash. What gives way.
I dream: this is not true, that I breathe sunlit rooms, that I live
off endless space. I love in fragments. They line up and line
up in waves. Now, I count differently, in so many winters.
Color comes into it: blue. I shift in passages of sleep. Dreams
of deep water work out the trouble—its aimless, heavy waves,
the girl with scales. Half human, half fish. An early story:
she walked in pain: how much love that meant, wordless, out
of her element. What I say and what I say. Divided angel,
quickening the ground.

Mike

do you remember, we had
the same enemies

the boys with shocks
of bangs, brown or

black or blond or red
their shirt tails

untucked, already a force
of fists and teeth

how names stuck, it was
third grade, 1968, and you were the new

the only black kid, Mike, do you remember
the lunch line of our religious school

we were surrounded, and we

were the same, and we
were not, *boy, girl, black, white,* both

unpopular, and when I could not stand
this anymore, the way they all surrounded

you, and I against them
with you

words, raw heart, raw nerve
for that moment

their stunned
little faces, no teacher anywhere

in sight, do you remember

we shared a table
do you remember calling me

that afternoon
and on the phone you asked

what was my house like, and parents

paced, so many steps beyond
the receiver, behind me

in a green bedroom
a pattern circling, wires humming

and I said *nothing*

what was *unwise*
quietly explained

later, a kind of lesson, the difference
between right and wrong

complex and rearranged, a story
of creation

no less
and what it meant to turn away

and Mike, how would you remember me

in that childhood town
of sticks and stones

how I went along
after all, divided

waving from a distance in my nice dress

Unspoken

> "Between 1882 and 1968, an estimated 4,742 blacks met their deaths at the hands of lynch mobs. As many if not more blacks were victims of legal lynchings (speedy trials and executions), private white violence...murdered by a variety of means in isolated rural sections...."
> —from "Hellhounds" by Leon F. Litwack, included in *Without Sanctuary: Lynching Photography in America*

of such news
no one ever said anything

in that childhood house

as if all that mattered were going to church
and folding napkins

so the seams wouldn't show

as if childhood itself were a matter of staying proper
and protected

as if everyone had a childhood like ours

supposedly was

with birthday cakes and ribbons galore, sweet
and simple

as if the woman who had come to work at that house for
    twenty-five years
with dignity

never minded accusations that were almost like family jokes
about petty theft

uttered once in a while

under my great aunt's breath, the door from the dining room
to the kitchen swinging shut

again and again, the dishes served

again and again—

how the woman who came to work never smiled

in those rooms—

the country she lived in, the country whose rules
about theft

I didn't know

In the Midst of Place, Thoughts on Juneteenth

"Show me the house I must still be living in...."
—Larry Levis, from section 4,
"Like the Scattered Beads of a Dime Store Rosary,"
"Elegy with an Angel at Its Gate"

This morning, the pale green bird among the branches of cedar

I have better learned how to see, the turning hands of the fringe
of leaves, the trace

of rain, evidence of light beaded at the tips, fanning out, layers
of skirts, layers

of shawls, the resin of the smell on my hands this morning,
the quiet web

of light on the backs of the grasses, along the bent and twisted
wire of fences surrounding

the garden, a wild rose tree growing out of

this home, here—shadows long

before me, and morning light, the gold-rose that spreads across
these foothills

light exposing the raw earth

clearcuts thickly surrounded by trees lined up like matches,
little swaths

of sprayed land, of Roundup land, blasts of dynamite,
    land of crow, of red tail hawk, of jay,

of pileated woodpecker ringing

the fallen trees with its beak, rainwater filling the hidden springs,

the creeks, the well filling for the use of this house, among other
    wells, the stories, the words,

the shadows that fill them

at the throats, at the roots, of the trees, the underground
    interlocking ways I can't see, and I am

here by way of others' plans making possible my own, and this
    home goes back

a long way, to other forests along a different coastline,
    a different name

for opportunity, claimed, cut down, Jamestown, English,
    Scotch Irish names given to me,

the portraits I passed as a child in those halls, following

a grandmother I adored

seeking the sounds of her house, the house of my mother,
    always, the sound of rain on tin,

the gaze of the crow in the rain, the voice of my grandmother,
    snapping beans, the woods hiding

the trace of a self

traces of stories—my grandmother's mother

born in the Shenandoah Valley, orphaned, capable, stitching

a child's scalp struck by a stone to stop the bleeding

    and still the vast European reach

of diseases, the former slave houses, corridors of sentiment

that backhanded wish, my hand

"Scurrying across a sheet of paper" because of and despite

what I have learned:

    daughter of daughter of daughter—

    the wild rose, the unbidden, thick-stemmed, red-leafed—

Armband Chorus of the American Dream

—after the death of Michael Jackson

we would walk through fire for our fathers
we say this still, we would
carry heavy loads, we would smile for the camera
from a very young age
we would not burden our mothers
who lean on us at funerals
in this white world
we would walk through fire
we are the boys
this is America
we are the boys no matter how old
we are by ourselves
we would walk through fire for our fathers
we would not burden our mothers who say
our fathers are going to kill us
maybe we have
the wrong fathers and maybe we are
the wrong sons
we try to fix things
in this white world
our mothers would watch the swing
of the belt, of the boot, they would bear it
unable to leave
we are the boys
growing up
strong

we hide things
in this white world
we walk through fire, we can do anything
in this white world
our fathers died a long time ago
in this white world
we are black we are
white
in this white world, our fathers
they live in our hearts
they leave us their success

Shriek

over and over I know there's a dog somewhere in a yard I cannot locate on the dark slope of that foothill west of me now dark against the burning light of a sun no longer visible behind the trees over and over I have asked about this sound I have called the neighbors (what must they think) they seem to hear nothing and I have heard children playing and talking along with the dog cries so nothing should be wrong should it the high-pitched chatter echoes against the walls of the mountains I have heard how the dog goes silent as I watch the moon change shape each night (I hope for him to be led kindly I hope for the warm windows of his dwelling place) this happens over and over as if it were normal as if there were no distress along with the normal sunset along with the normal phases of the moon as if I am imagining things as if there is a missing code of conduct held by many others so they do not hear and so I do not understand

To You Who Found My Brother

Man in the field

you saw

what we could not,
after a week of looking,

and after that, not even
at the morgue could it
be borne.

He had planned the way
to an open pasture,
carefully leaving
his keys behind.

I know nothing
about you, but think
of what you carried—

he was more than that

last place on earth,
that dark map,

my brother,

and so
are we, so

are you.

Traveling

Along a coastal road, where I have not been for years, this
    particular whiteness breaks out of

turquoise, dark blue, shadows of violet, before disappearing
    again behind switchbacks,

a well of branches and dense green leaves. Sudden sun blinding
    a curve.

Sometimes the sky opens up, and waves hit, the horizon

at a slant, the pure moon-pull of it. I am years

away from the sea town I am remembering:

its wind-driven beach, sand shifting like smoke. The ground

unsettled, forming flocks of edges I briefly mistook for birds

that morning. Pale wings and beaks vanishing

out of themselves into something else

indistinguishable from air,

memory:

My own brother's

eyes, dark brown. And only in my saying here

no more, they are.

The Coffin of Emmett Till

> "I cry every day. But I cry as I move."
> —Mamie Till-Mobley

It is the silence
the barn door slammed shut
on a child in the middle of the night
the way the river water
rushes, covers what it covers
the way the heavy lid
stays shut
stays shut
until she refuses
silence
the awful lid
her child shut
beneath the moon, the ink-black water
that covers
what they did—it took more
than one beating, it took the fan
of a cotton gin
it took a knot of barbed wire
it took
the fear of big white men
yet still
he floated up
and she refuses silence
and she names him
and she refuses
to bury this
boy beneath the lid
he's traveled far
all the way back

from any hole in Mississippi, far
from orders of that government
and it can't just be
a leaden box
of stones or bricks
it can't just be
a trick
with no boy there
on that returning train
a box big enough to fill
three graves
she refuses, she unseals
she needs to know
the way the distant river
and its little markets,
little houses,
sheriffs with their guns and beer and pop
the official state itself
Mississippi
would cover him
she would know
this is her child
from his well-made
slender
ankle bones
his sturdy legs
none of Emmett's body scarred
all the way up
up to his chin
she needs to
face him
face him

open it

Stem of Nests

Demeter in November

—for the mothers

Morning is first a trace of stars
moon and tree-shadow
then cloud.

The mountains fill with release
the last crimson and gold
before the erasure of leaves.

And when they fall
scattering the lines of the house
these afternoons

I will see my child

beneath the white oak trees
years ago, on a blanket the color of honey.

Nest

low on the bough
a gathering
of leaves and lichen

      interwoven
vessel, well
of being
seen

      at a glance

settled
in the wind

      the dark bird there

beneath the branches
over wild iris
blackberry thorn

where I will
not go

      shadows crossing
           and crossing

the tops of the trees
alder, fir, and oak

                giants,
    the circling
                span
of wings

November Return

Pregnant and dark
black bear
in the cold
predawn
orchard

slow moving
through rain,
beneath the backs
of mountains

smelling
and eating
invisible pears
fallen
to the ground—

right instinct
filling itself
in time

shadow upon shadow
without an individual name,
hiding places—
she, these

in the distance

clear my mind
when I cannot
sleep.

Migration in Changing Climates

The trees breathe—

green reaches, ragged
with lichen

over a road furrowed with rain
each winter, branches

the nest

of shadows, its weave
of grasses and leaves,

wings

branching a sky within

night and day,
a white oak stirring

our atmosphere, currents
of trees, migrations

out of time, spaces
abandoned, taken

releasing
the gold and crimson

tanager's song, recurring
attention, all we have,

unseasonably
early, this spring—

An Aspect of Theater

> —after *An Experiment on a Bird in the Air Pump*,
>   a painting by Joseph Wright of Derby, 1768

> "A travelling scientist is shown demonstrating the formation of a vacuum by withdrawing air from a flask....Air pumps were developed in the 17th century and were relatively familiar by Wright's day. The artist's subject is not scientific invention, but a human drama in a night-time setting."
>   —notes on the painting published by
>   The National Gallery, London

    the subject
        that bird is dying
in absolute stillness
behind all of the conversation
one wing extended, white plumes of its breast, and
    slowly but surely
some witnesses suffer
their high suffering pure
fascination, while others
tenderly
look away
    from what might be
"violent and irregular Convulsions"
proving "Respiration is so necessary to the Animals,
that Nature hath furnish'd with Lungs"
    their faces glowing
in eighteenth-century flame
illuminating the bird in its transparent
cage,

                the light in those faces
light shaped by dark
shaped by the candle and the moon
brow robe shoulder cheek
        I imagine the child
who did look
would never forget
this feeding
of vision
on a table laden
with a human skull
in its own glowing glass, the bird
rare "though common birds like sparrows
would normally have been used"
        meanwhile
the lid of glass above the bird
still held shut
or almost lifted
by the traveling scientist's delicate grip
between thumb and forefinger
        the bird

its beak
its eyes still open

Subject Matter

> "You say that you could never eat a snake?/ Had you been there,
> mademoiselle, in seventy one/this zoo would seem the freshest
> of buffets./ We too would have denied it of ourselves/ but war is
> turpentine that strips the gloss."
> —from "Madame L. Describes the Siege of Paris"
> by Beth Ann Fennelly

an unexpected intimacy, this carrying away, what I
hardly see while driving mid-afternoon, what must be
a hawk with a smaller creature clutched
in its talons, though for me it is the tension of pure flight
of shadows while knowing
it is not simply
one body curved beneath another's
outstretched wings, the silent passage
over the green pastures toward
a grove of trees,
protective—
    and this wingless creature
the size of a small dog or cat,
what must it see
for the first time, what cold
rush of air,
how it must forget its pain
in the faraway, the shock of grip
that takes it there—
    and I think of the stillness
of the Woman at the Window
a model for Degas

in a city under siege, his conveyance of her
in essence of oil, like watercolor, paint
"drained of its oil," her dark dress, possible lace
at her wrist, her neck, the hands on her lap in repose
I think, except that fist of light, the fingers
of her right hand closed, lit
by whiteness,
the whiteness of the sky
in that window, the ragged blur
of ochre windows beyond the sash
     emptiness filled
how light the cloth cap covering her hair
must be, transparent,
how the light appears to shine
     against the gravity
of her seated form,
how it was recounted
Degas paid her
with a "hunk of meat ... 'which she
fell upon, so hungry was she,
and devoured it raw,'"
how we   observe the effect
    of her restraint, Degas' experiment,
        his eyesight ever failing, lifting her

out of time just before

Parvin Butte

I cannot see it, stripped
of pine and brush

its raw sides
spilling rock and dust

ragged cavity, pocked
and sinking deeper

seams of narrow road
digging in, winding around

and around, its little puffs of smoke
its loopholes, rules and laws

this thirty million dollar
"pile of rocks"

the "ditch" around it, cannot see
who named a tributary

"ditch," a mountain
"pile of rocks"

to which they could do
anything, good-for-

nothing
cannot see

what's happening
in the courts of law

"what the land is good for"
all that money

among the gardens'
paid-for taxes, farms and houses

so nearby, invisible
the screech owl's call

these spring nights
turtles slipping into water

from their stones, no wiser
for the ditch they're in, breeding grounds

for them, for salmon, water filling wells
beneath the ground

of sudden blossoms
moss and lichen

what feeds the yearling deer
curled among the lavender

the bells of snow queen, the cache of iris
For Sale signs everywhere

another spring
opening, undone

Volatilization in Cedar Valley

Chemicals of war
drift over this green

nook of farms and schools,
2, 4-D, chloride, among

others, imprecise
blends in their vats

hovering overhead,
the grease and fumes

exacting profit
from a simple register

protected by law
in the name of marketable trees—

but no one can make the deer
value the fruit,

fallen
untouched,

what seeps in

to the gut of a dog
roused from his kennel

or a boy running to look
for TV adventure,

the bright stream passing
beneath dying branches, soaking

soil and root, ready for rising
in the indefinite

weather-shifts,

the bright stream
singing as never before,

carrying everything.

Drowning in Space

sometimes in the summer of fires

beneath stars
open rims of constellations

I pace the dark kitchen, calm myself
in a rigid chair

the hook in my back
invisible

the place where I secretly thrash, earth
dry as a bone—as if

my neck had gills, sharp black slashes

pulsing out of their element
for what can't get in, the shut system

a sky full of wonder
I cannot feel

the air in its transparency
life consumed by smoke

a burning I cannot see
behind the blue mountains

air officially
deemed hazardous—

as a child I used to dream about
the cutting off of the line (who would do it?)

from the mother ship

among the galaxies
where we would float and float

away
in a vast light

Stem of Belongings

Praise Songs for a House

Like dreams or prayers, rough-hewn
jackknife carvings beneath the sills
and wedged in corners, fastened thin
plaques of pine the size
of large index cards, recordings
against rough cedar

    walls, ways of remembering
the wolf tracking scent
of a path along an imagined
forest, the trees blunt outlines, faded
green, jagged cones, and the soft blue
that somehow lasted, nocturnal sky
as if lit up by moon

    and in another
world, along another window, a bear rising,
salmon clasped
between its jaws, shaggy
forelegs lifted above the ground
of river waves, etched clouds
 above the catch of fish, a ragged sky

    and by the wood-burning
stove, a curving snake, cut in relief
from a split of wood
I will not burn, letting
it guard there, tapered, reminding me of gifts,

      of other children
who lived here, perhaps one who wove
the garland still hanging in my room,
dry pale-yellow blooms

      grapevine, clover, marigold,
heather blossom, all that grew here.

Keeping the Fires

in spring frosts

what could not be
warded off

all night he watched

guarding the blooms

small pockets
of warmth

breathing
and vanishing

measures of light

Ekphrasis

    —for Aurelia

You said it is like a dream
here, in these northern woods, late summer
light pouring over the stones
of the river, the river
our walk, the evening birds returning
from the shadows of white pine, cedar, and birch
along the banks, wood warblers feeding as if on air amidst
the blue hum and chirr
of insects, their nearly
invisible wings, glints
stirring above the water
stirring
the shadows
of fractured stones—that music
like a dream
you said, and I follow, I know you are choosing
to share this world with me, we are choosing this path

I am now describing, where we walked together, where
a part of me stays, as if
our childhood behind us
such a path in the place of absences
is possible
beloved sister   and we can go
anywhere

Waking Vision

they open their eyes
all of the little webs
membranes of rain
and light the instant
of that slant of morning
sun, countless matrices
seaming
various ways
the narrow distances between
telephone wires strung
one above the other
like the lacing of nerves
like the lacing of rain
and of light
crossing over
glances bordering winter
gardens, the mesh of gates
and windows, frames
uneven
interweaving
just now
shimmering
in this one way
and they open their eyes
the road black with rain
to the distances
they open their eyes
spinning
body after body
of earth and light and darkness and rain

Belonging

from your kitchen, near the side
of your dying dog

where you sit, listening—

you will remember the sigh
of a struck match

in winter for however long
you live

as if it were shelter
light reflected

against the wood burning stove

hidden springs
feeding the dark well

the home you keep

the ground you lean against

What Stays

    —for Lisa Rosen (1958 - 2008)

I note
savory and *sweet*,
my friend using such discretion,
leaning over baked goods
displayed behind glass,
considering. I still see her
at the coffee shop
where we brought our stash
of poems every Wednesday
morning for years, until she could no more.
Her words in my kitchen
particular, the salt next to the honey,
references to blossom
beside her brave gifts,
giant coffee cups for fullness, splashes
of blueberry and strawberry-rose
a surprise
pulled
from bright wrapping papers
she wished for me
over a Greek meal despite
the hard days. The value of sun.
The value
of entering this world
however we could,
winter
or spring, books
I keep opening.

Witness of Roses

> —in memory of Michael and his Roadside Roses

skin of petals lined, traces
like crepe, like the way
my face and hands are changing

fluted yellow cup
losing its surfaces,
pink sips
of light, and blood-red
extravagance, like a party
that has nothing to do
with me

I am this
gathering of good intentions,
brief purchases above the traffic of I-5
where a man sits in a beat-up lawn chair
next to a plastic bucket of flowers, selling them
in almost any weather, roses
of unknown origin, I never ask

and on days when I don't buy
to bring sweetness to a shelter
he doesn't have, I catch his eye, smile, drive past, and
      sometimes
he waves "oh hey!" but I keep driving, and the next time I see

bright scatterings in place of a man and a chair, a rose placed in the hollow of a steel post, a road barrier, petals strewn on the ground, red, yellow, pink,

what falls on my table

Stem of Prayers

....we will go planting

Make poems
seed grass
feed a child growing
build a house....

Wherever
I walk
I will make

—Muriel Rukeyser, from "Wherever"
included in **The Collected Poems of Muriel Rukeyser**

poem in the dark

it comes out of storms

these trees
how they are leaving
grounded, flung

slowly breaking
the shape
of mountains

the afternoon
before
a flock of robins
hidden among
white oak branches
revealed

their sudden
thousand cries
shrill
in the warm air

before the rains
rising and falling

praise to the green
turn of the boughs
the wrists and hands

of the cedar
fragrant
tipped with light

reflecting the trees
of rain I remember

Prayer for the Black Bears, Lost Valley

May you loathe
the scent of us

raw torn smells

the
wild we live from

may you
     go away

heard at night
too close, primaeval

mothering
cracking the branches

back into the honey
of the nameless

deep
green
mountains

Stories of the Black Ware Seed Jar

—after a seed jar created by R. Diane Martinez

I have been through fire.
My form is fixed,
smoke-dark,
patterns of wing,
beak, thunder, and eye,
the storm of birds
chasing each other,
energies of life.
Cool and dry,
burnished
with stone,
I recall patience
through winter,
through wind,
through the rains
that fill the arroyos.
I absorb, hold
what stirs, rattles
like prayers,
like snakes,
awaiting release until
they pour my gifts
into the field again,
what you imagine—
where I began,
seed after seed,

fire becoming
field,
blossom and grain
and all of the voices
therein.

The Possible Stories of Trees

the mouths
and shawls of them
    fringes
of form, form sometimes
the elbows and eyes, sometimes
the sockets, the shaggy wings
of them, sometimes broken
stumps, the shouldering
of birds
the bodies of trees
sometimes
clasping
each other
still growing
however they can
tracking the paths
of light
invisible
lichens
absorbing
the air, sleeving
branches of trees, the mosses
tracking years of north
along the trunks of trees

beyond speech
    how long will they be
who shapes become
their roots buried

in the stones and the clay
among veins of dark
springs and quartz
hidden seams
and stories
beneath the visible stones—

this time the deer is suddenly
      rising
from shadows, the ground cold
with rain, her dark eyes
white-rimmed, the white
patch of her throat
fully seeing

beyond reason   so suddenly close
      and she rises, she
            does not turn away—

What Must Be True

keep the strange book you have chosen
open

your willingness
toward its emptiness

not yours
and yours

the table before you
nothing

suspended
over the distances

your desire of signals
your willingness toward

what may live
in darkness

fragment after
fragment

you can keep

what may become
hidden tracks

unbound

    the running deer
    beyond the window   her dark

what can never
    be found

    the green world
        of that window

    signaling

    the bright road
    of rain

    leading to the house
    not here but made

    of that rain
    the door left open

    at the bottom of the childhood stairs

    so you might see her

    the sharpness
    of light

    what may stay with you

light deepening

the shadows of branches
you cannot see

shaping the field of the page
the imprint

the calling

what must be true

      given

you keep following

To Be Greeted at the River

the gray unpromising
cold becoming
     your folded wings
your back
curved
over the rushing waters
I call you
blessing
     the slightest turn
of your head toward me
the sharp
edge of your long beak
against
the river and traffic
ebbing and surging
echoing stone
and concrete
unceasing
hollow throats
so many
gone
dear brother dear friend dear
unknown
and where do I go
but away
so as not to disrupt
your attention
for what might feed you
for what might live

beneath the cold
grasses and waters
in this dark-green
November light
where I step back
not to lay this to waste—
      vast
      blue wingspan
      my eyes have surely seen

* * *

Prayer for Heaven

May it hold the sounds
of the raw seams of our world,
our difficult heart, the borders
always at war.
May it hold mercy.
May it never be
above and beyond
blossoms
scattering.
May it gather the blossoms beyond
the dark wall, on every side
revealing
an opening.
May it discover new names.
May heaven be generous, may
its own burning
sky,
its seraphim of infinite
moons and suns,
include every loss, even
the loneliness of the bones of a dog
floating
among the miracles of space
before the anonymous fall, the abandoned vessel's
fiery descent, everything
gone wrong, may it include even
the loneliness of the dog.

May it hold in its eye
the deep blue
dream we keep trying to tell—
how the light falls apart,
then is saved
no matter what happens,
again and again, may heaven
be the singing, and may we be
       forever changed.

Notes on poems from *Stem of Us*

In the Midst of Place, Thoughts on Juneteenth

Juneteenth is known as Juneteenth Independence Day, Freedom Day, and Emancipation Day. It is an American holiday commemorating the June 19, 1865 announcement of the abolition of slavery in the state of Texas, two and a half years after President Lincoln's Emancipation Proclamation. Juneteenth is the "oldest known celebration commemorating the ending of slavery in the United States," a celebration with the mission to "promote and cultivate knowledge and appreciation of African American history and culture." (**History of Juneteenth**, juneteenth.com)

Excerpts from "Elegy with an Angel at Its Gate" from **Elegy**, by Larry Levis, © 1997. Reprinted by permission of the University of Pittsburgh Press.

The Coffin of Emmett Till

Emmett Louis Till (July 25, 1941-August 28, 1955) was fourteen years old when, in the summer of 1955, he visited family members in Mississippi from his hometown of Chicago. It was during this visit that two white men abducted him from his relatives' home. They asserted that he had flirted with a white woman. Emmett's mutilated body was found in the Tallahatchie River three days later. Had his mother Mamie Till-Mobley complied with authorities, her son would have been hastily buried in Mississippi; had she complied with authorities, the box that contained his body, which was transported by train to Chicago at her insistence, would never have been opened. Emmett Till's open-casket funeral was attended and recorded by tens of thousands of witnesses, and galvanized the Civil Rights Movement.

"I cry every day. But I cry as I move." Words by Mamie Till-Mobley spoken during an interview in December 1996 with Devery S. Anderson, author of **Emmett Till: The Murder That Shocked the World and Propelled the Civil Rights Movement**.

An Aspect of Theater,
    after *An Experiment on a Bird in the Air Pump*

"violent and irregular Convulsions" proving "Respiration is so necessary to the Animals, that Nature hath furnish'd with Lungs": Robert Boyle, from his notes on "Experiment 41," included in **New Experiments Physico-Mechanicall, Touching The Spring of the Air, and its Effects (Made, for the most part, in a New Pneumatical Engine)**, published in 1660.

"though common birds like sparrows would normally have been used": from notes on the painting published by the National Gallery, London, United Kingdom.

Subject Matter

"drained of its oil," and "hunk of meat ... 'which she fell upon, so hungry was she, and devoured it raw'": Text including words attributed to the artist Walter Sickert, in a statement accompanying the painting **Woman at the Window** by Hilaire-Germain-Edgar Degas (1834-1917), exhibited at The Courtauld Gallery, London, United Kingdom.

The excerpt from the poem "Madame L. Describes the Siege of Paris" is used with permission by Beth Ann Fennelly.

Epigraph to Stem of Prayers

Excerpts from the poem "Wherever" by Muriel Rukeyser are used with permission by William L. Rukeyser. The poem appears in **The Collected Poems of Muriel Rukeyser** published by the University of Pittsburgh Press.

Acknowledgements

Grateful acknowledgement to the following journals
and anthologies where these poems first appeared:

"Translation": **The Whistling Fire**
"Prayer for Heaven": **Canary**
"Stories of the Black Ware Seed Jar": **Canary**
"November Return" (published under the title "November"):
   Turtle Island Quarterly
"Volatilization in Cedar Valley": **Turtle Island Quarterly**
"The Coffin of Emmett Till": **Of Course, I'm a Feminist!**
   and **Sisyphus**
"Before Nightfall": **What the River Brings: Oregon River Poems**
"Waking Vision": **The Poeming Pigeon: Poems from the Garden**
"What Must Be True": **Transit, WITS Anthology**

Thank you to Hervé Sauquet & Jürg Schönenberger for the use of different images of the flower on the cover and throughout the book. I was excited to learn of this 'first flower' — the ancestor of all flowers. I immediately felt its connection to **Stem of Us**.

With thanks to Erik Muller, Maxine Scates, Alison Townsend, Michael Spring, and Marion Malcolm for their careful readings of earlier drafts of this manuscript. Their insights and encouragement were invaluable.

About the Author

Carter McKenzie's work has appeared in journals and anthologies, including *What the River Brings: Oregon River Poems, Canary, Sisyphus, Turtle Island Quarterly, The Berkeley Poets Cooperative: A History of the Times,* and the poetry anthology *Of Course, I'm a Feminist!* She lives in a small community in Western Oregon's Middle Fork Willamette watershed region. Carter is an active member of the Springfield-Eugene Chapter of SURJ (Showing Up for Racial Justice). *Stem of Us* is her second full-length book of poetry.